AN INTRODUCTION TO FRACTIONS

Math Workbooks Grade 6
Children's Fraction Books

Speedy Publishing LLC
40 E. Main St. #1156
Newark, DE 19711
www.speedypublishing.com

FRACTIONS

EXERCISE 1

What is the fraction of the shaded part?

1) 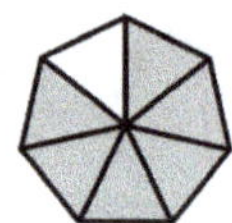 ______

2) 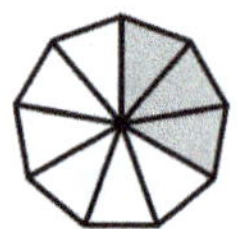 ______

3) 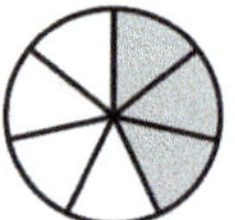 ______

4)  ______

5) 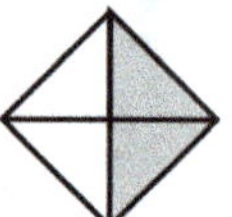 ______

6) 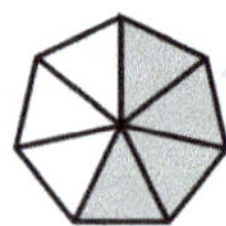 ______

7)  ______

8)  ______

9) 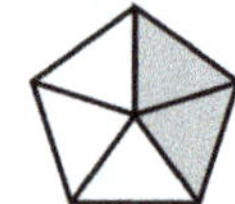 ______

10)  ______

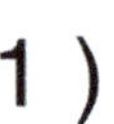
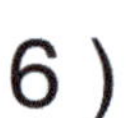

EXERCISE 2

What is the fraction of the shaded part?

1) 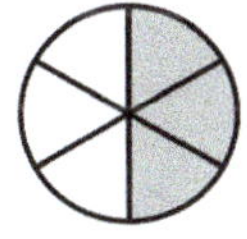 ______

2) 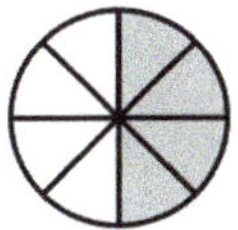 ______

3) 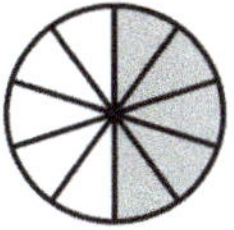 ______

4)  ______

5)  ______

6)  ______

7) 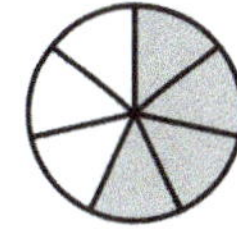 ______

8) 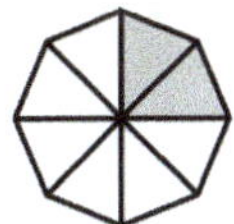 ______

9) 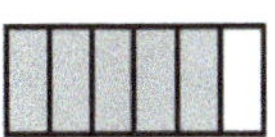 ______

10) 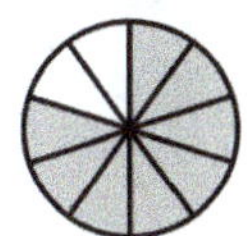 ______

EXERCISE 3

What is the fraction of the shaded part?

1) 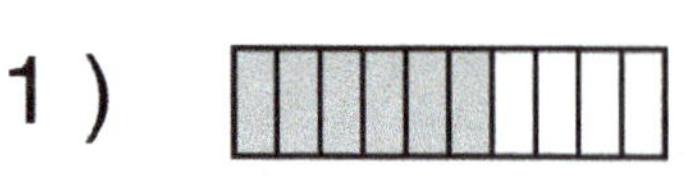 ______

2) 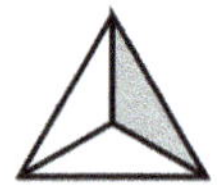 ______

3) 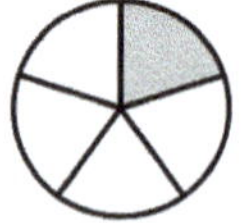 ______

4) 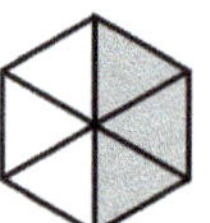 ______

5) 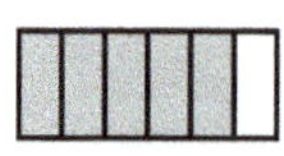 ______

6) 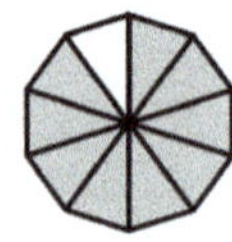 ______

7) ______

8) 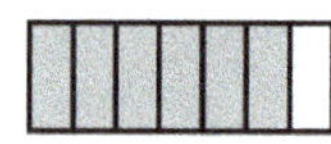 ______

9)  ______

10)  ______

EXERCISE 4

What is the fraction of the shaded part?

1) 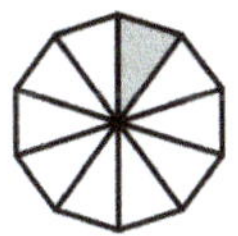 ______

2)  ______

3) 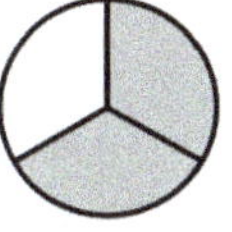 ______

4) 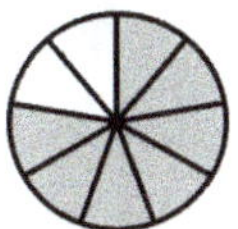 ______

5) 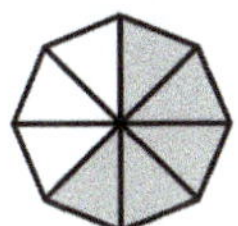 ______

6) ______

7) 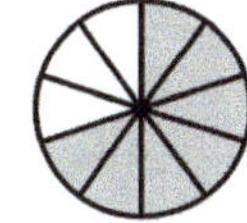 ______

8)  ______

9) 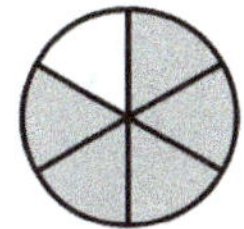 ______

10) 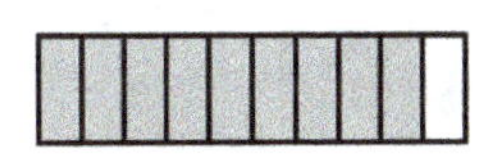 ______

EXERCISE 5

What is the fraction of the shaded part?

1) 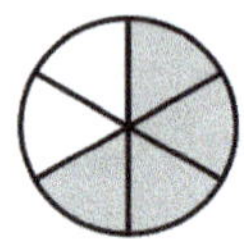 ______

2) 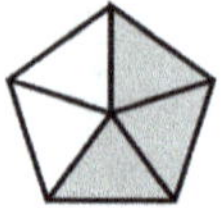 ______

3) 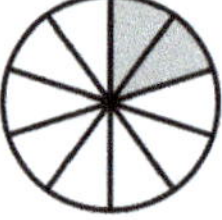 ______

4) 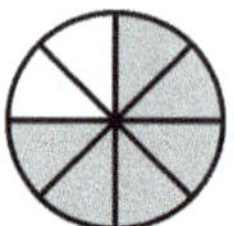 ______

5) 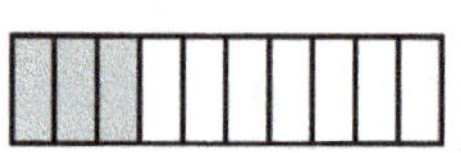 ______

6)  ______

7) 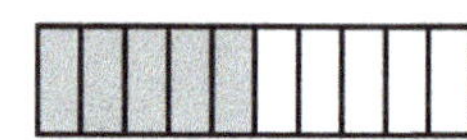 ______

8)  ______

9) 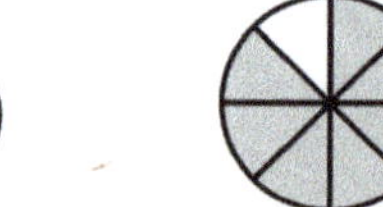 ______

10) 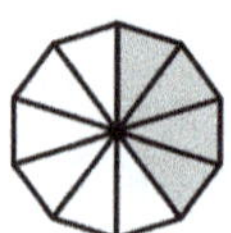 ______

EXERCISE 6

What is the fraction of the shaded part?

1) 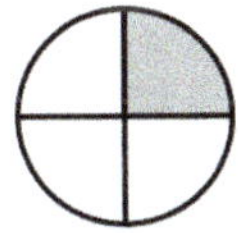 ________

2) 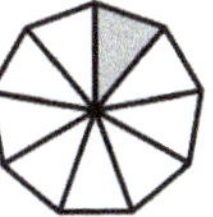 ________

3) 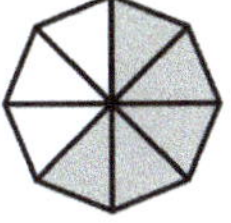 ________

4) 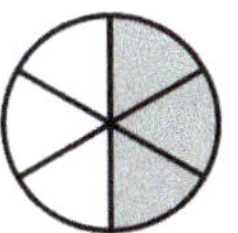 ________

5) 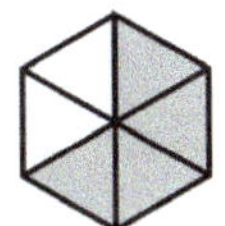 ________

6)  ________

7) ________

8) 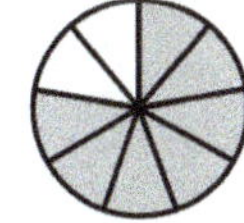 ________

9) 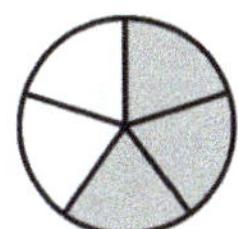 ________

10) 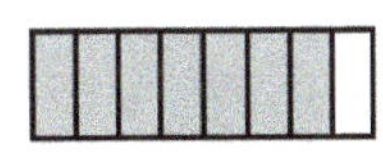 ________

EXERCISE 7

What is the fraction of the shaded part?

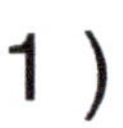

1) 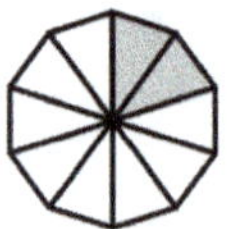 ______

2) 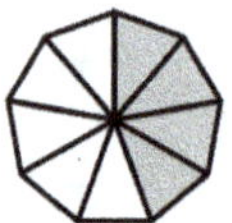 ______

3) 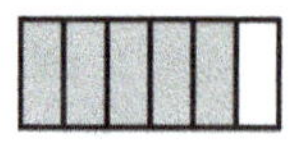 ______

4) 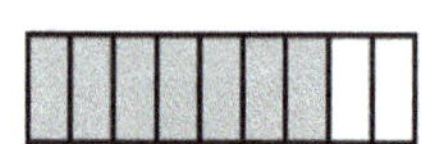 ______

5)  ______

6)  ______

7) 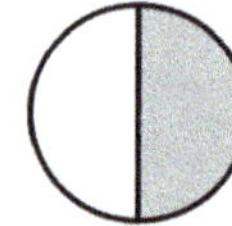 ______

8)  ______

9) 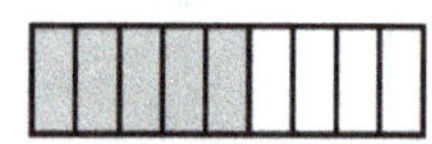 ______

10)  ______

EXERCISE 8

What is the fraction of the shaded part?

1) 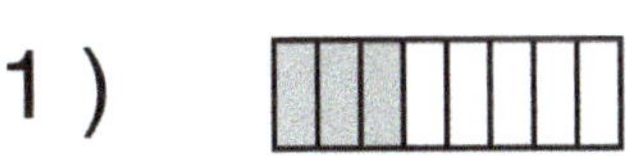 ______

2)  ______

3) 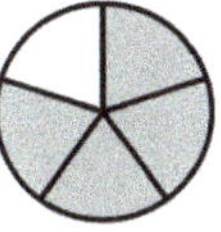 ______

4) 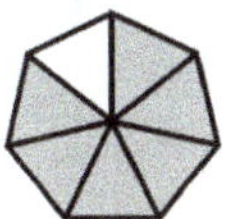 ______

5) 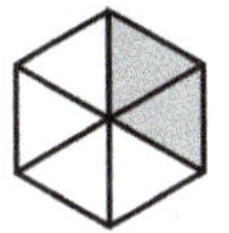 ______

6) 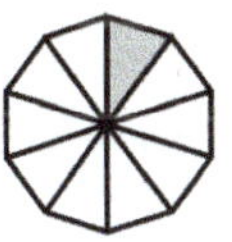 ______

7) 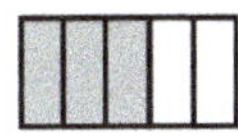 ______

8) 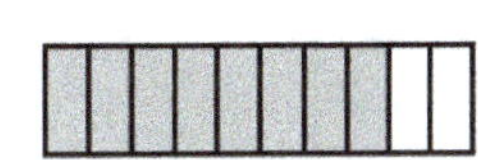 ______

9) 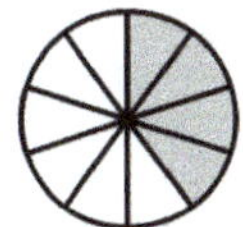 ______

10) 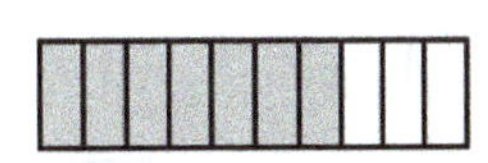 ______

EXERCISE 9

What is the fraction of the shaded part?

1) 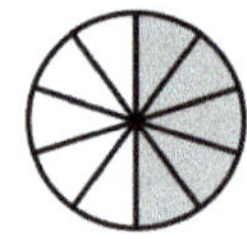 ______

2) 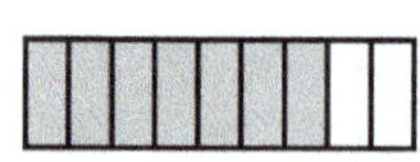 ______

3) 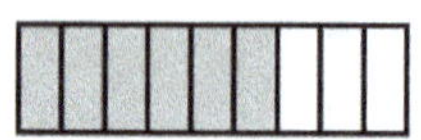 ______

4)  ______

5) 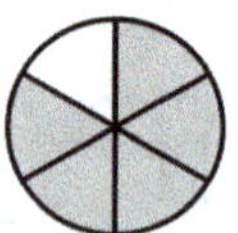 ______

6) 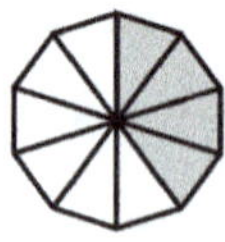 ______

7) 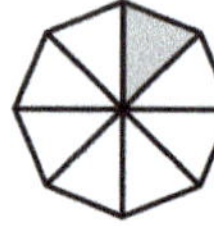 ______

8)  ______

9) 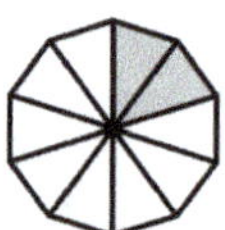 ______

10)  ______

EXERCISE 10

What is the fraction of the shaded part?

1)  ______

2)  ______

3) 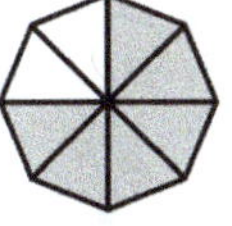 ______

4) 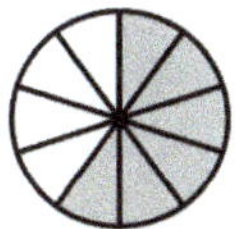 ______

5) 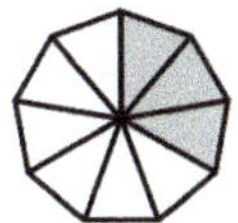 ______

6) 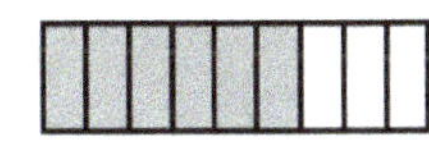 ______

7) 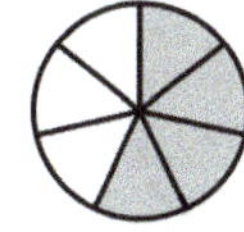 ______

8) 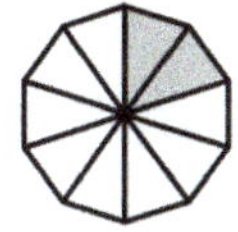 ______

9) 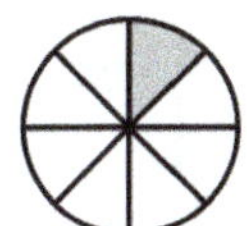 ______

10) 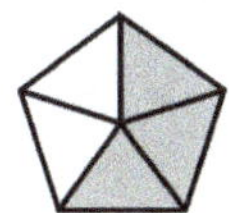 ______

EXERCISE 11

What is the fraction of the shaded part?

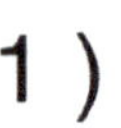

1) 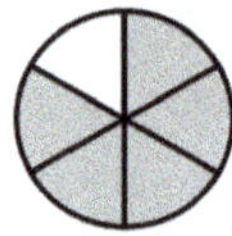 ______

2) 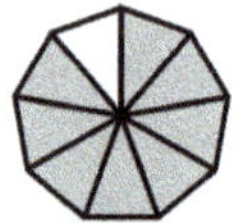 ______

3) 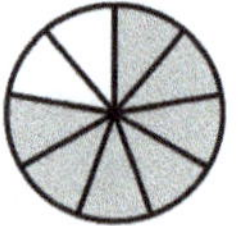 ______

4) 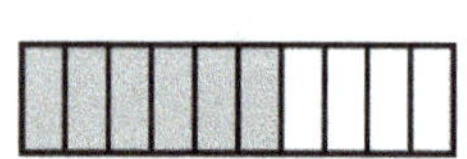 ______

5) 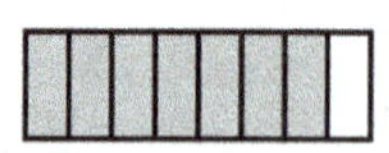 ______

6) 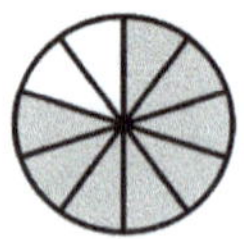 ______

7) 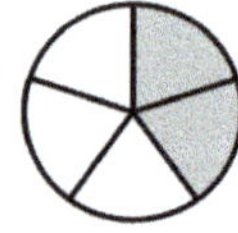 ______

8) 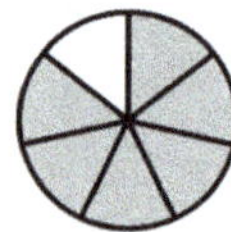 ______

9) 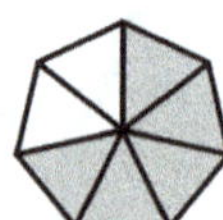 ______

10)  ______

EXERCISE 12

What is the fraction of the shaded part?

1) 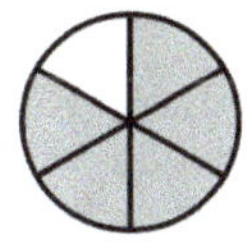 ______

2) 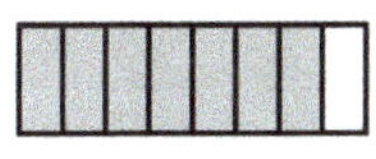 ______

3) 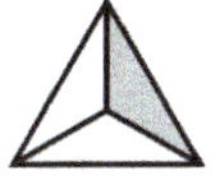 ______

4) 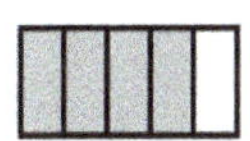 ______

5) 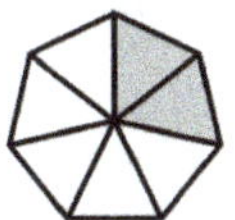 ______

6) 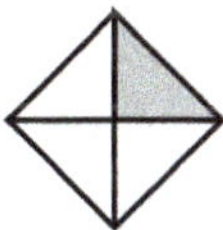 ______

7) 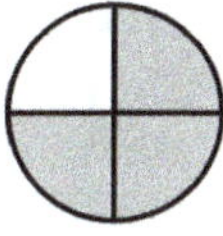 ______

8) 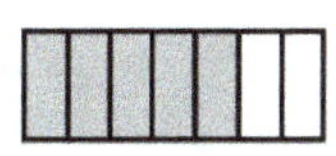 ______

9)  ______

10) 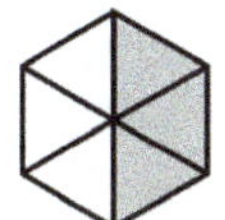 ______

EXERCISE 13

What is the fraction of the shaded part?

1) 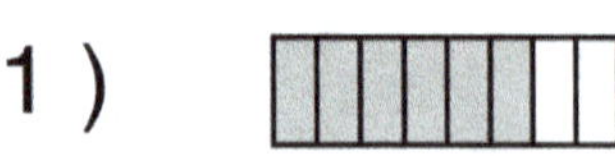 ________

2) 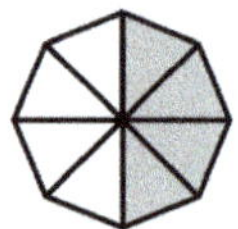 ________

3)  ________

4)  ________

5) 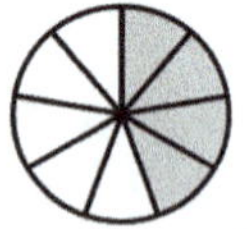 ________

6) 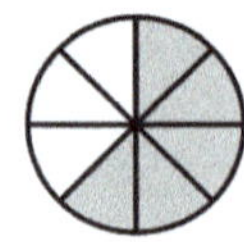 ________

7)  ________

8) 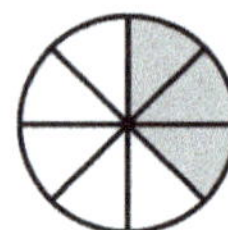 ________

9) 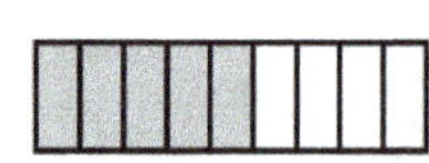 ________

10) 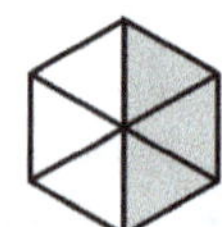 ________

EXERCISE 14

What is the fraction of the shaded part?

1) 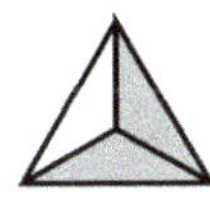 ________

2) 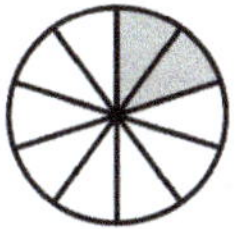 ________

3) 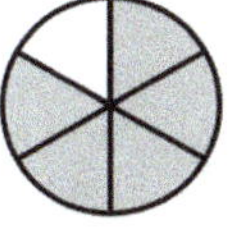 ________

4) 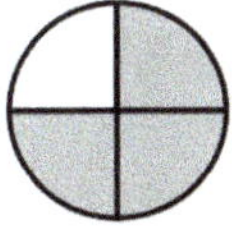 ________

5)  ________

6) 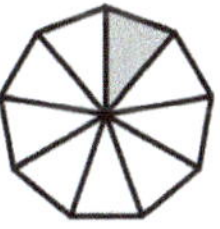 ________

7) 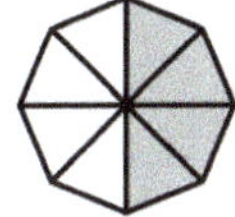 ________

8)  ________

9) 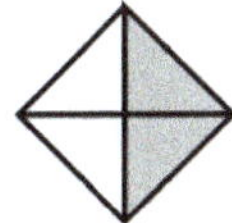 ________

10) 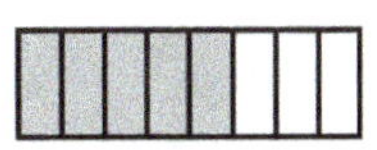 ________

EXERCISE 15

What is the fraction of the shaded part?

1) 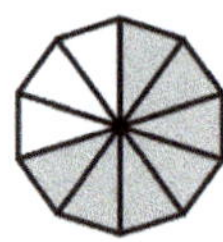 ______

6) 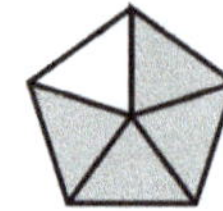 ______

2)  ______

7)  ______

3) 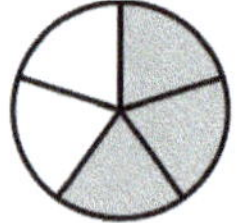 ______

8) 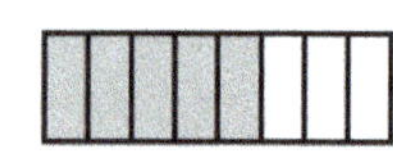 ______

4) 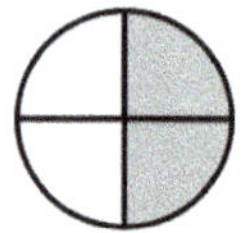 ______

9) 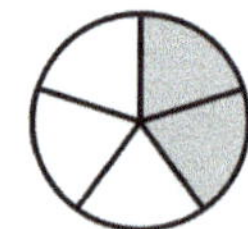 ______

5) 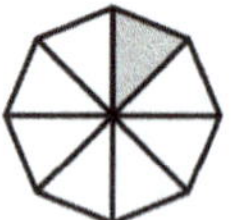 ______

10)  ______

EXERCISE 16

What is the fraction of the shaded part?

1) 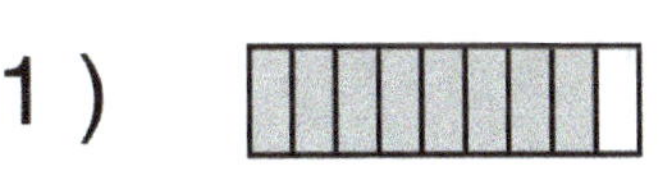 ________

6) 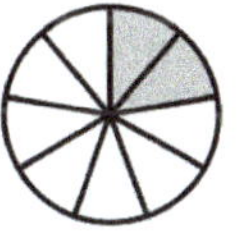 ________

2) 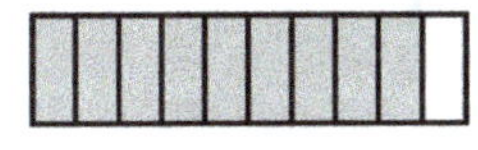 ________

7)  ________

3) 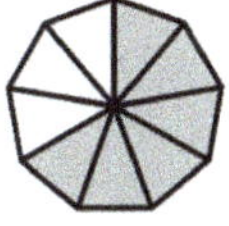 ________

8) 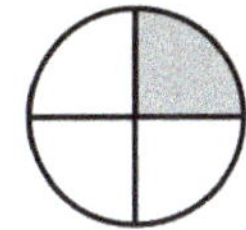 ________

4) 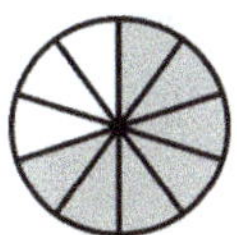 ________

9)  ________

5) 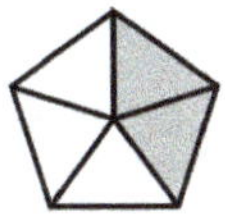 ________

10)  ________

EXERCISE 17

What is the fraction of the shaded part?

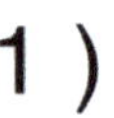

1) 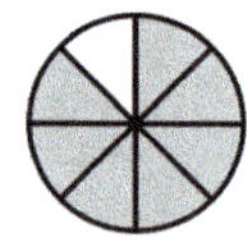 ______

6) 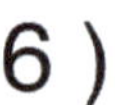  ______

2)  ______

7) 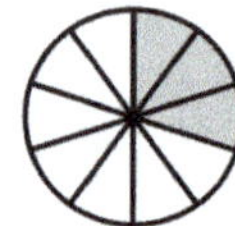 ______

3) 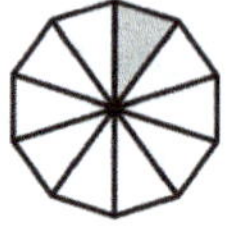 ______

8)  ______

4)  ______

9)  ______

5) 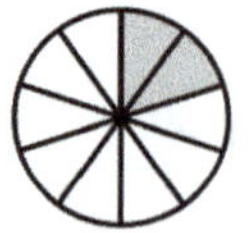 ______

10)  ______

EXERCISE 18

What is the fraction of the shaded part?

1)  ______

2) 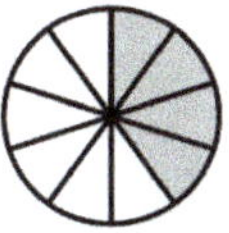 ______

3)  ______

4) 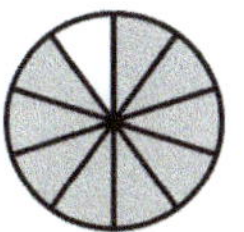 ______

5) 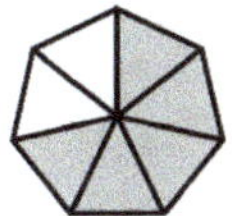 ______

6)  ______

7) 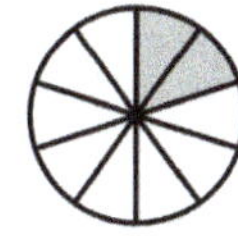 ______

8) 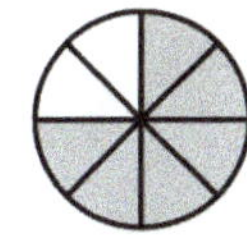 ______

9) 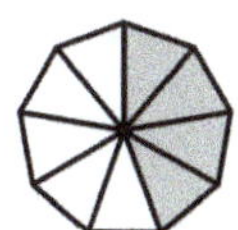 ______

10)  ______

EXERCISE 19

What is the fraction of the shaded part?

1)  ______

2) 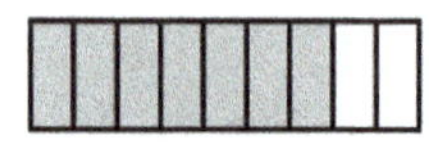 ______

3) 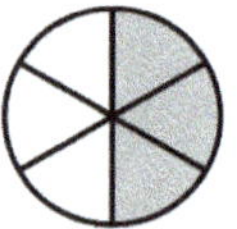 ______

4) 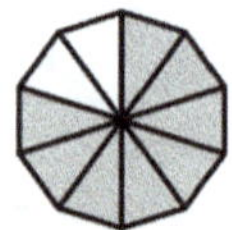 ______

5)  ______

6) 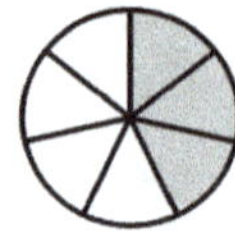 ______

7) 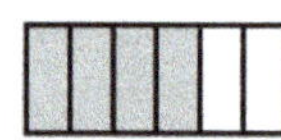 ______

8) 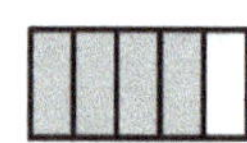 ______

9) ______

10) 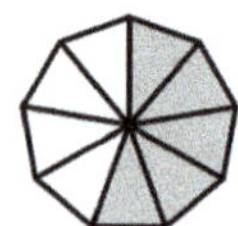 ______

EXERCISE 20

What is the fraction of the shaded part?

1) 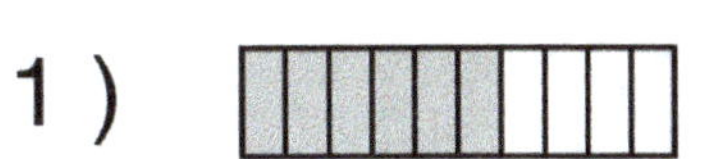 ________

2)  ________

3)  ________

4) 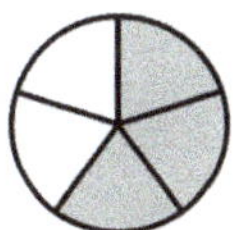 ________

5) 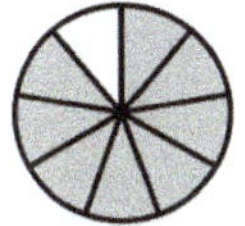 ________

6) 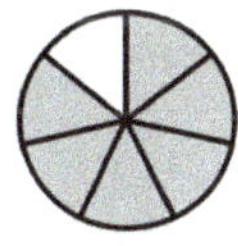 ________

7) 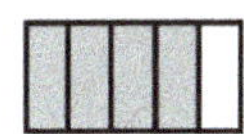 ________

8) 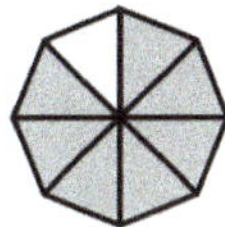 ________

9)  ________

10) 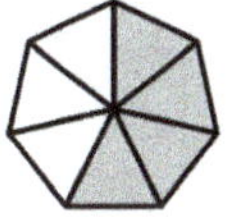 ________

EXERCISE 21

Shade the figure with the indicated fraction.

1) 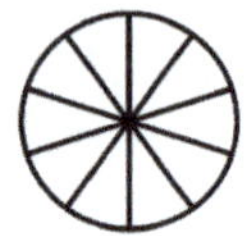 $\frac{8}{10}$ ______

2) 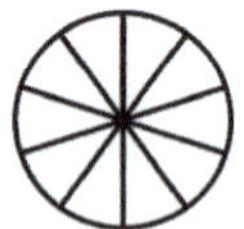 $\frac{9}{10}$ ______

3)  $\frac{2}{6}$ ______

4) $\frac{3}{6}$ ______

5) 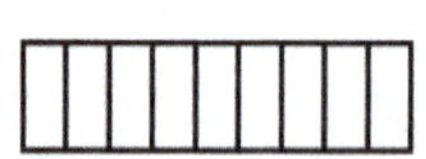 $\frac{1}{9}$ ______

6)  $\frac{3}{8}$ ______

7) $\frac{1}{3}$ ______

8) 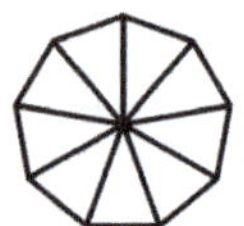 $\frac{8}{9}$ ______

9)  $\frac{4}{10}$ ______

10)  $\frac{1}{2}$ ______

EXERCISE 22

Shade the figure with the indicated fraction.

1) 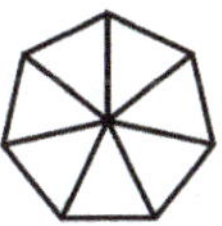 $\frac{6}{7}$ ________

2) $\frac{5}{9}$ ________

3) 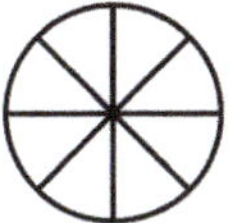 $\frac{7}{8}$ ________

4) 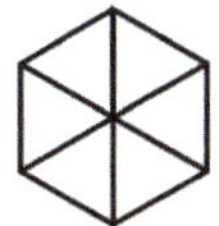 $\frac{4}{6}$ ________

5)  $\frac{1}{10}$ ________

6) 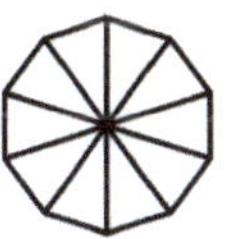 $\frac{7}{10}$ ________

7) $\frac{1}{3}$ ________

8)  $\frac{7}{9}$ ________

9)  $\frac{6}{8}$ ________

10) 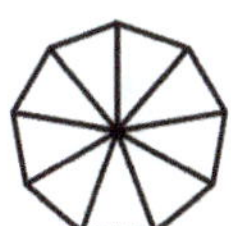 $\frac{1}{9}$ ________

EXERCISE 23

Shade the figure with the indicated fraction.

1)	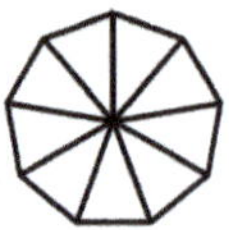	$\frac{4}{9}$ ______	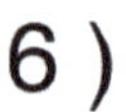 6)		$\frac{8}{10}$ ______
2)		$\frac{2}{8}$ ______	7)		$\frac{7}{9}$ ______
3)		$\frac{1}{9}$ ______	8)		$\frac{4}{10}$ ______
4)		$\frac{5}{9}$ ______	9)		$\frac{2}{6}$ ______
5)		$\frac{2}{9}$ ______	10)		$\frac{3}{4}$ ______

EXERCISE 24

Shade the figure with the indicated fraction.

1) 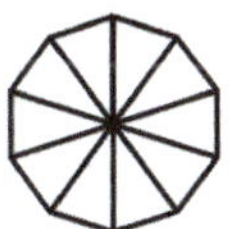 $\frac{6}{10}$ ______

2) $\frac{2}{5}$ ______

3) 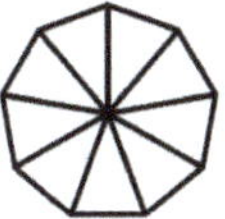 $\frac{6}{9}$ ______

4) 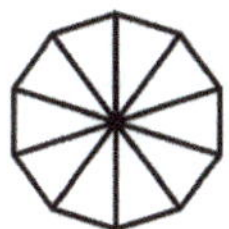 $\frac{5}{10}$ ______

5)  $\frac{3}{4}$ ______

6)  $\frac{3}{7}$ ______

7)  $\frac{8}{9}$ ______

8)  $\frac{4}{7}$ ______

9)  $\frac{2}{8}$ ______

10) $\frac{2}{6}$ ______

EXERCISE 25

Shade the figure with the indicated fraction.

1)  $\frac{3}{4}$ ______

2) 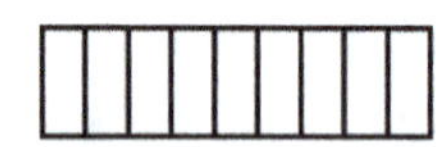 $\frac{8}{9}$ ______

3)  $\frac{6}{9}$ ______

4) 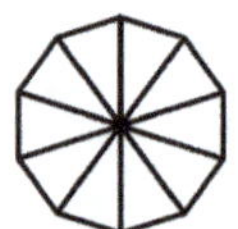 $\frac{6}{10}$ ______

5)  $\frac{1}{9}$ ______

6)  $\frac{1}{7}$ ______

7) 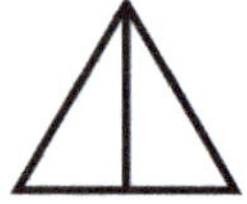 $\frac{1}{2}$ ______

8)  $\frac{1}{6}$ ______

9)  $\frac{2}{3}$ ______

10)  $\frac{2}{7}$ ______

EXERCISE 26

Shade the figure with the indicated fraction.

1) $\frac{1}{3}$ ________

2) $\frac{2}{3}$ ________

3) $\frac{2}{10}$ ________

4) $\frac{1}{5}$ ________

5)  $\frac{5}{10}$ ________

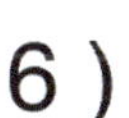

6) 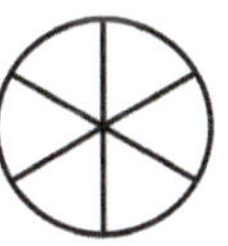 $\frac{2}{6}$ ________

7) $\frac{5}{7}$ ________

8) $\frac{8}{9}$ ________

9) $\frac{4}{5}$ ________

10) 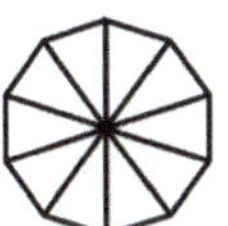 $\frac{3}{10}$ ________

EXERCISE 27

Shade the figure with the indicated fraction.

1)	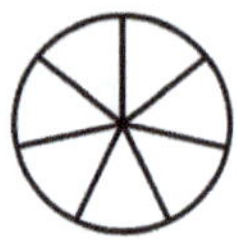	$\frac{1}{7}$	6) 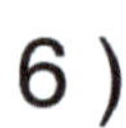	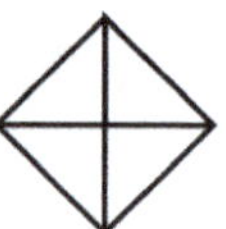	$\frac{3}{4}$
2)		$\frac{3}{5}$	7)		$\frac{7}{8}$
3)		$\frac{6}{7}$	8)	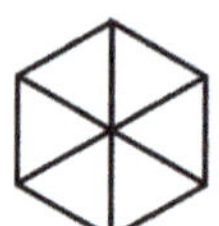	$\frac{3}{6}$
4)		$\frac{5}{7}$	9)		$\frac{6}{8}$
5)		$\frac{1}{5}$	10)		$\frac{1}{9}$

EXERCISE 28

Shade the figure with the indicated fraction.

1) 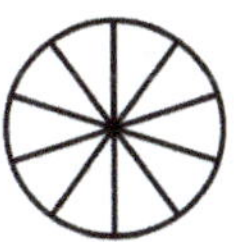 $\frac{3}{10}$ ______

2) $\frac{2}{5}$ ______

3) 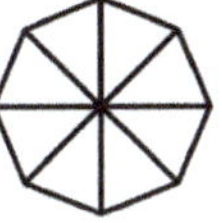 $\frac{4}{8}$ ______

4) 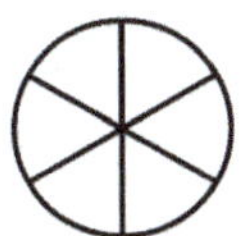 $\frac{3}{6}$ ______

5)  $\frac{6}{8}$ ______

6)  $\frac{1}{2}$ ______

7) $\frac{5}{6}$ ______

8)  $\frac{4}{7}$ ______

9) 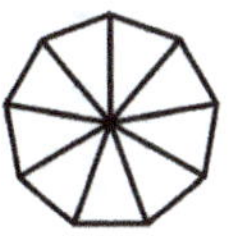 $\frac{2}{9}$ ______

10) 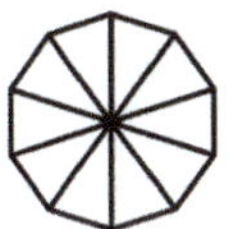 $\frac{6}{10}$ ______

EXERCISE 29

Shade the figure with the indicated fraction.

1) $\frac{5}{7}$ __________

2) 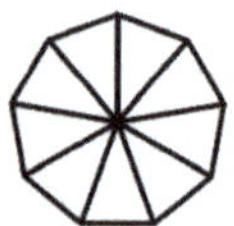 $\frac{2}{9}$ __________

3)  $\frac{5}{9}$ __________

4)  $\frac{2}{3}$ __________

5)  $\frac{7}{8}$ __________

6)  $\frac{3}{4}$ __________

7) 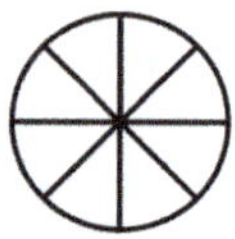 $\frac{5}{8}$ __________

8)  $\frac{1}{3}$ __________

9)  $\frac{2}{7}$ __________

10)  $\frac{1}{10}$ __________

EXERCISE 30

Shade the figure with the indicated fraction.

1) 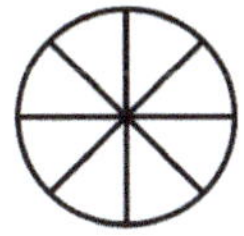 $\frac{7}{8}$ ____

2) $\frac{4}{9}$ ____

3) 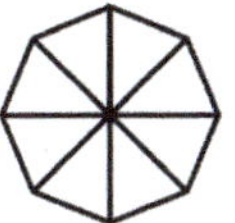 $\frac{4}{8}$ ____

4) $\frac{2}{5}$ ____

5) $\frac{3}{6}$ ____

6)  $\frac{8}{10}$ ____

7) 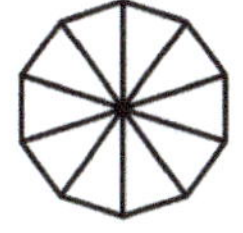 $\frac{5}{10}$ ____

8) 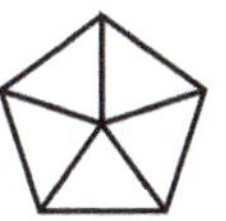 $\frac{4}{5}$ ____

9)  $\frac{3}{10}$ ____

10) 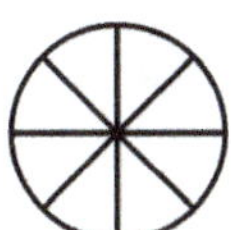 $\frac{2}{8}$ ____

EXERCISE 31

Shade the figure with the indicated fraction.

1)  $\frac{2}{4}$

6) 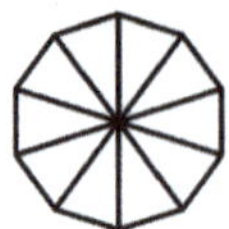 $\frac{9}{10}$

2)  $\frac{3}{4}$

7) 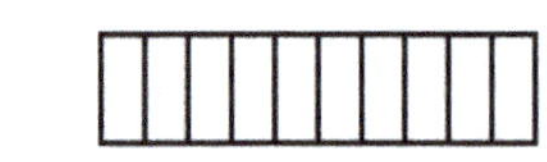 $\frac{7}{10}$

3)  $\frac{1}{10}$

8)  $\frac{6}{9}$

4)  $\frac{2}{10}$

9)  $\frac{5}{10}$

5)  $\frac{4}{5}$

10)  $\frac{3}{9}$

EXERCISE 32

Shade the figure with the indicated fraction.

1)  $\frac{4}{9}$ ______

2) $\frac{4}{7}$ ______

3)  $\frac{3}{10}$ ______

4) 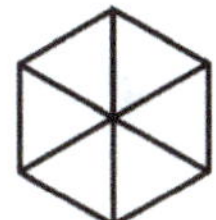 $\frac{2}{6}$ ______

5)  $\frac{3}{9}$ ______

6) $\frac{1}{8}$ ______

7) $\frac{9}{10}$ ______

8) 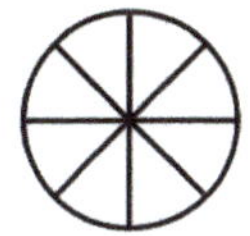 $\frac{5}{8}$ ______

9)  $\frac{8}{10}$ ______

10)  $\frac{4}{10}$ ______

EXERCISE 33

Shade the figure with the indicated fraction.

1) $\frac{6}{9}$ ______

2) $\frac{1}{4}$ ______

3) 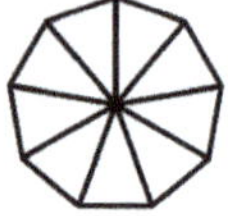 $\frac{1}{9}$ ______

4) $\frac{3}{4}$ ______

5)  $\frac{7}{8}$ ______

6)  $\frac{2}{4}$ ______

7)  $\frac{2}{3}$ ______

8) 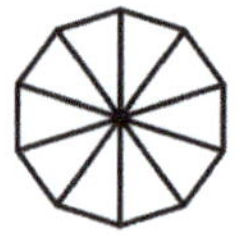 $\frac{7}{10}$ ______

9)  $\frac{3}{9}$ ______

10) 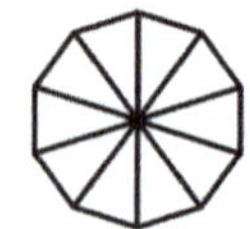 $\frac{3}{10}$ ______

EXERCISE 34

Shade the figure with the indicated fraction.

1) 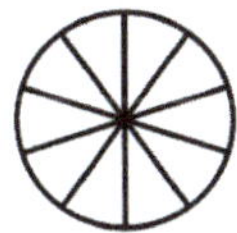 $\frac{8}{10}$ ______

2) $\frac{6}{9}$ ______

3) $\frac{4}{6}$ ______

4) $\frac{1}{2}$ ______

5)  $\frac{4}{9}$ ______

6) 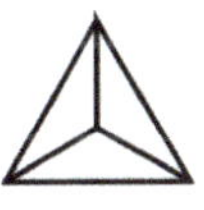 $\frac{1}{3}$ ______

7) $\frac{2}{7}$ ______

8)  $\frac{1}{7}$ ______

9)  $\frac{3}{9}$ ______

10)  $\frac{6}{8}$ ______

EXERCISE 35

Shade the figure with the indicated fraction.

1) $\frac{1}{9}$ ______

2)  $\frac{8}{9}$ ______

3)  $\frac{6}{9}$ ______

4) $\frac{6}{8}$ ______

5) $\frac{1}{6}$ ______

6) 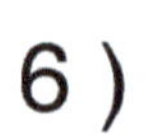  $\frac{1}{7}$ ______

7) 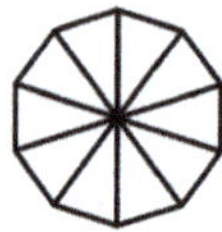 $\frac{3}{10}$ ______

8)  $\frac{1}{4}$ ______

9) $\frac{4}{6}$ ______

10) $\frac{3}{4}$ ______

EXERCISE 36

Shade the figure with the indicated fraction.

1)  $\frac{3}{5}$ ____

2) $\frac{4}{9}$ ____

3)  $\frac{1}{10}$ ____

4) 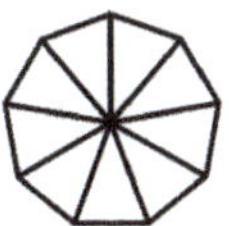 $\frac{3}{9}$ ____

5) 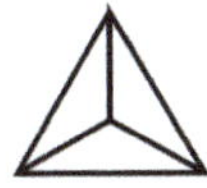 $\frac{2}{3}$ ____

6)  $\frac{3}{7}$ ____

7)  $\frac{8}{10}$ ____

8) 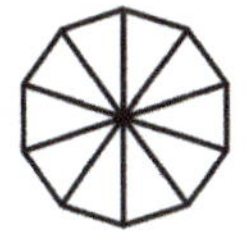 $\frac{6}{10}$ ____

9)  $\frac{1}{7}$ ____

10)  $\frac{1}{2}$ ____

EXERCISE 37

Shade the figure with the indicated fraction.

1) 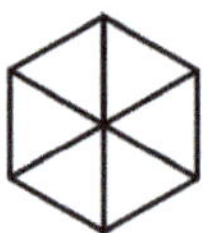 $\frac{5}{6}$ ______

2)  $\frac{5}{7}$ ______

3) 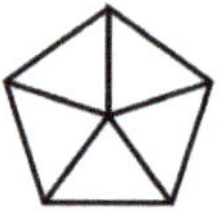 $\frac{1}{5}$ ______

4) $\frac{1}{2}$ ______

5)  $\frac{4}{7}$ ______

6) 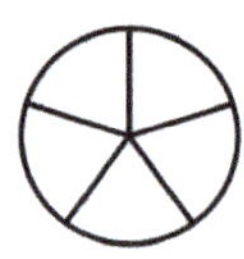 $\frac{2}{5}$ ______

7) 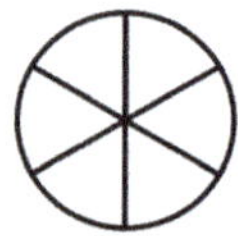 $\frac{4}{6}$ ______

8) 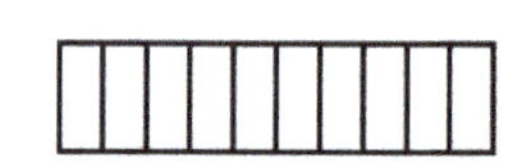 $\frac{4}{10}$ ______

9) 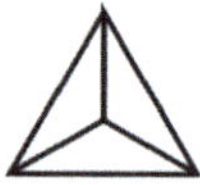 $\frac{2}{3}$ ______

10)  $\frac{9}{10}$ ______

EXERCISE 38

Shade the figure with the indicated fraction.

1) $\frac{2}{8}$ ________

2)  $\frac{4}{8}$ ________

3)  $\frac{7}{9}$ ________

4) 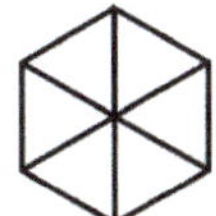 $\frac{4}{6}$ ________

5)  $\frac{6}{9}$ ________

6) 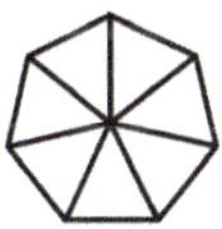 $\frac{1}{7}$ ________

7) $\frac{1}{8}$ ________

8)  $\frac{3}{5}$ ________

9) $\frac{3}{10}$ ________

10) $\frac{6}{10}$ ________

EXERCISE 39

Shade the figure with the indicated fraction.

1) 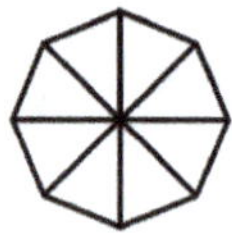 $\frac{1}{8}$ ______

2) $\frac{6}{9}$ ______

3)  $\frac{5}{10}$ ______

4)  $\frac{5}{7}$ ______

5)  $\frac{6}{7}$ ______

6) 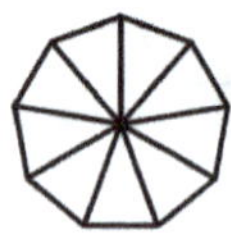 $\frac{2}{9}$ ______

7)  $\frac{4}{8}$ ______

8) 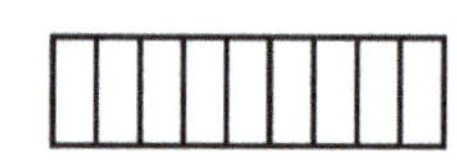 $\frac{8}{9}$ ______

9)  $\frac{5}{8}$ ______

10)  $\frac{4}{10}$ ______

EXERCISE 40

Shade the figure with the indicated fraction.

1)  $\frac{2}{6}$ ______

2) 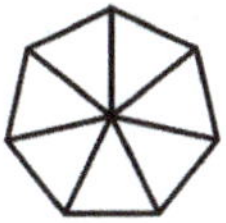 $\frac{5}{7}$ ______

3) 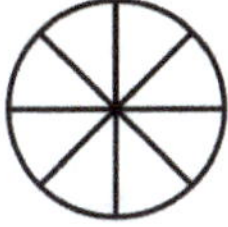 $\frac{2}{8}$ ______

4) 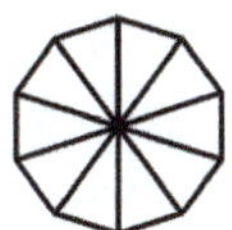 $\frac{1}{10}$ ______

5) 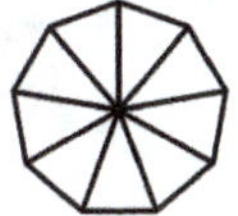 $\frac{7}{9}$ ______

6) 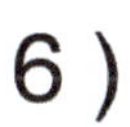 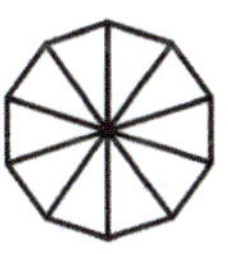 $\frac{7}{10}$ ______

7) $\frac{2}{7}$ ______

8)  $\frac{1}{8}$ ______

9)  $\frac{9}{10}$ ______

10) $\frac{1}{5}$ ______

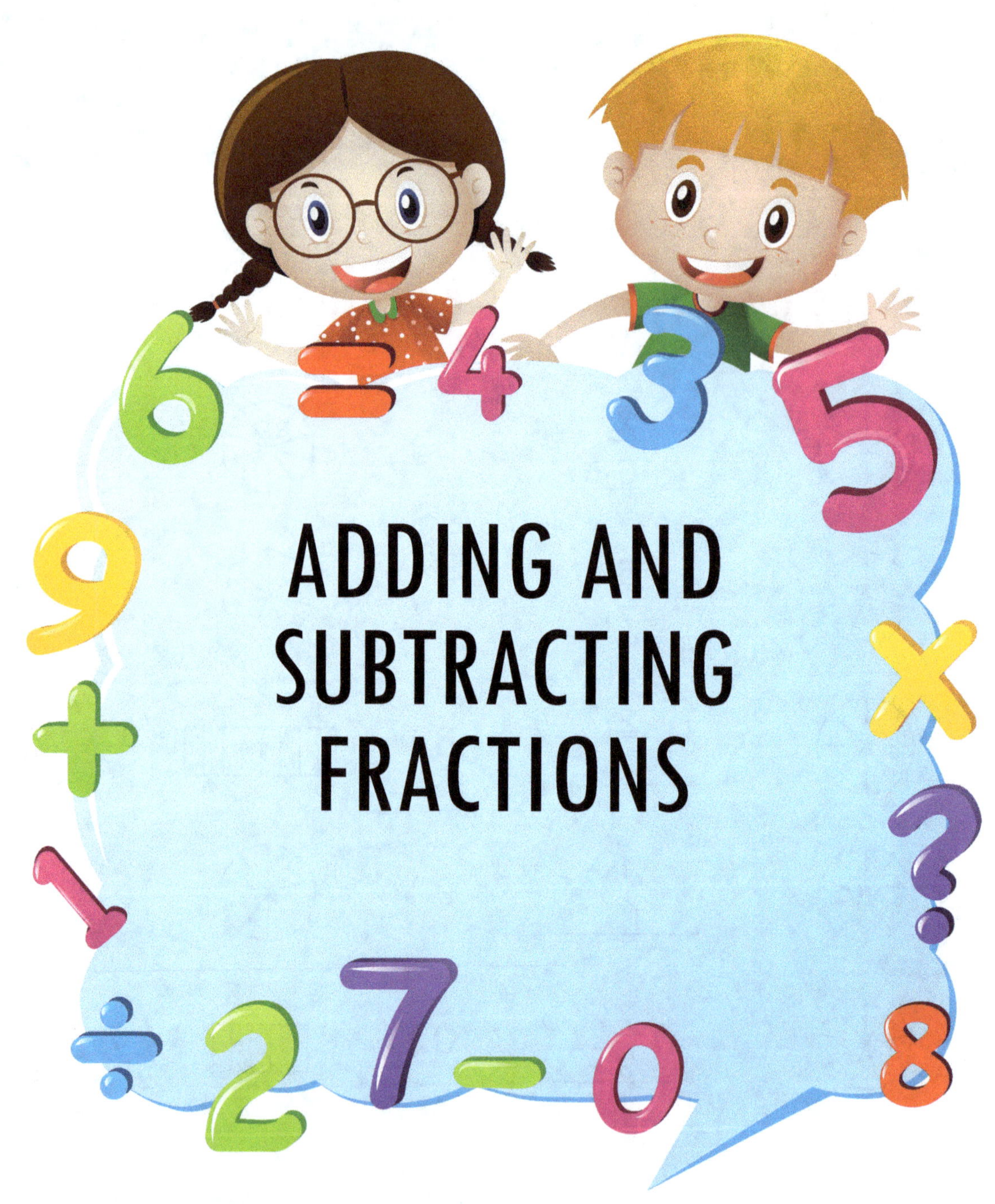

ADDING AND SUBTRACTING FRACTIONS

EXERCISE 1

1) $\frac{1}{4} + \frac{2}{4} =$

2) $\frac{2}{9} + \frac{6}{9} =$

3) $\frac{2}{12} + \frac{2}{12} =$

4) $\frac{2}{5} + \frac{2}{5} =$

5) $\frac{1}{12} + \frac{7}{12} =$

6) $\frac{1}{10} + \frac{1}{10} =$

EXERCISE 2

1) $\frac{1}{6} + \frac{3}{6} =$

2) $\frac{1}{3} + \frac{1}{3} =$

3) $\frac{4}{12} + \frac{7}{12} =$

4) $\frac{1}{4} + \frac{2}{4} =$

5) $\frac{3}{12} + \frac{6}{12} =$

6) $\frac{4}{10} + \frac{4}{10} =$

EXERCISE 3

1) $\frac{1}{4} + \frac{2}{4} =$

2) $\frac{2}{9} + \frac{6}{9} =$

3) $\frac{2}{12} + \frac{2}{12} =$

4) $\frac{2}{5} + \frac{2}{5} =$

5) $\frac{1}{12} + \frac{7}{12} =$

6) $\frac{1}{10} + \frac{1}{10} =$

EXERCISE 4

1) $\frac{8}{10} - \frac{1}{5} =$

2) $\frac{2}{4} - \frac{1}{5} =$

3) $\frac{7}{10} - \frac{2}{4} =$

4) $\frac{4}{5} - \frac{1}{2} =$

5) $\frac{4}{5} - \frac{3}{4} =$

6) $\frac{1}{2} - \frac{3}{10} =$

EXERCISE 5

1) $\frac{8}{10} - \frac{2}{4} =$

2) $\frac{4}{5} - \frac{4}{10} =$

3) $\frac{3}{5} - \frac{1}{2} =$

4) $\frac{2}{3} - \frac{1}{2} =$

5) $\frac{1}{2} - \frac{1}{5} =$

6) $\frac{1}{2} - \frac{1}{4} =$

EXERCISE 6

1) $\frac{5}{10} - \frac{1}{3} =$

2) $\frac{3}{5} - \frac{2}{10} =$

3) $\frac{1}{2} - \frac{1}{4} =$

4) $\frac{2}{3} - \frac{1}{2} =$

5) $\frac{9}{10} - \frac{1}{3} =$

6) $\frac{1}{2} - \frac{2}{10} =$

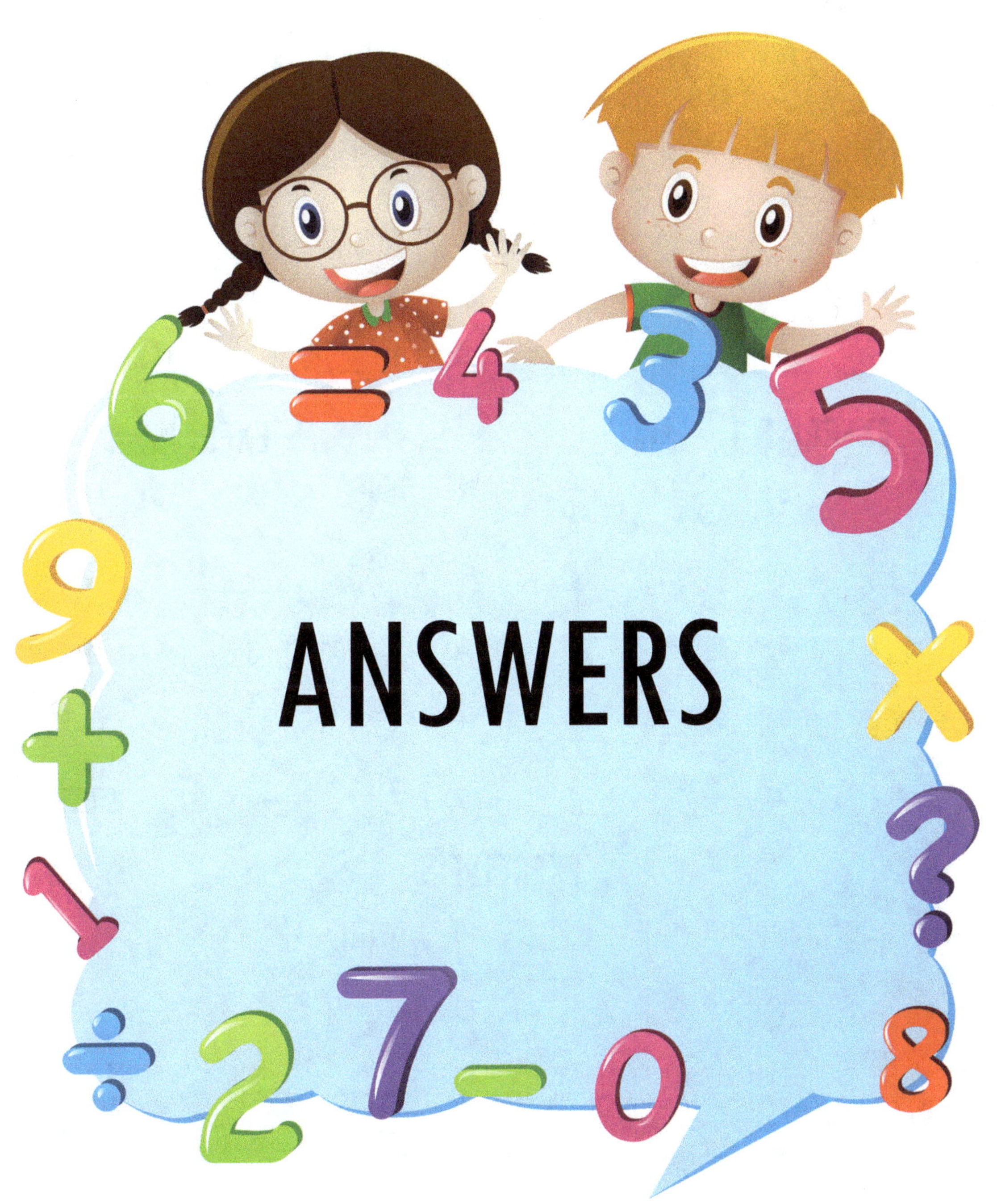
ANSWERS

EXERCISE 1

1) $\frac{6}{7}$
2) $\frac{3}{9}$
3) $\frac{3}{7}$
4) $\frac{5}{10}$
5) $\frac{2}{4}$
6) $\frac{4}{7}$
7) $\frac{3}{4}$
8) $\frac{1}{6}$
9) $\frac{2}{5}$
10) $\frac{7}{8}$

EXERCISE 2

1)  $\frac{3}{6}$
2) $\frac{4}{8}$
3) $\frac{5}{10}$
4) $\frac{1}{6}$
5) $\frac{2}{10}$
6) $\frac{3}{9}$
7) $\frac{4}{7}$
8) $\frac{2}{8}$
9) $\frac{5}{6}$
10) $\frac{8}{10}$

EXERCISE 3

1) $\frac{6}{10}$
2) $\frac{1}{3}$
3) $\frac{1}{5}$
4) $\frac{3}{6}$
5)  $\frac{5}{6}$
6) $\frac{9}{10}$
7) $\frac{7}{8}$
8) $\frac{6}{7}$
9) $\frac{5}{8}$
10) $\frac{2}{10}$

EXERCISE 4

1) $\frac{1}{10}$
2) $\frac{1}{5}$
3) $\frac{2}{3}$
4) $\frac{7}{9}$
5) $\frac{5}{8}$
6) $\frac{1}{2}$
7) $\frac{7}{10}$
8) $\frac{2}{9}$
9) $\frac{5}{6}$
10) $\frac{9}{10}$

EXERCISE 5

1) $\frac{4}{6}$
2) $\frac{3}{5}$
3) $\frac{2}{10}$
4) $\frac{6}{8}$
5) $\frac{3}{10}$
6) $\frac{4}{7}$
7) $\frac{5}{10}$
8) $\frac{1}{4}$
9) $\frac{7}{8}$
10) $\frac{4}{10}$

EXERCISE 6

1) $\frac{1}{4}$

2) $\frac{1}{9}$

3) 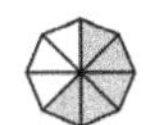 $\frac{5}{8}$

4) $\frac{3}{6}$

5) $\frac{4}{6}$

6) 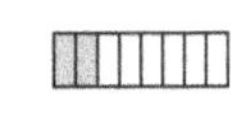 $\frac{2}{8}$

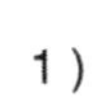

7) $\frac{2}{5}$

8) $\frac{7}{9}$

9) $\frac{3}{5}$

10) $\frac{7}{8}$

EXERCISE 7

1)  $\frac{2}{10}$

2) $\frac{4}{9}$

3) $\frac{5}{6}$

4) $\frac{7}{9}$

5) 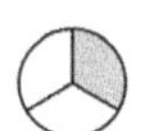 $\frac{1}{3}$

6) $\frac{2}{9}$

7) $\frac{1}{2}$

8) 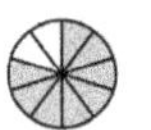 $\frac{8}{10}$

9) $\frac{5}{9}$

10) $\frac{4}{5}$

EXERCISE 8

1) $\frac{3}{8}$

2) $\frac{7}{8}$

3)  $\frac{4}{5}$

4) 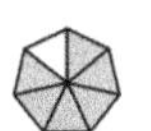 $\frac{6}{7}$

5) 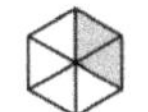 $\frac{2}{6}$

6) $\frac{1}{10}$

7) $\frac{3}{5}$

8) $\frac{8}{10}$

9) $\frac{4}{10}$

10) $\frac{7}{10}$

EXERCISE 9

1) 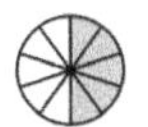 $\frac{5}{10}$

2) $\frac{7}{9}$

3) $\frac{6}{9}$

4) $\frac{3}{6}$

5) $\frac{5}{6}$

6) $\frac{4}{10}$

7) $\frac{1}{8}$

8) $\frac{1}{4}$

9) $\frac{2}{10}$

10) $\frac{1}{5}$

EXERCISE 10

1)  $\frac{1}{10}$

2)  $\frac{2}{3}$

3)  $\frac{6}{8}$

4)  $\frac{6}{10}$

5) 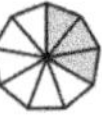 $\frac{3}{9}$

6)  $\frac{6}{9}$

7) 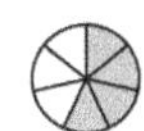 $\frac{4}{7}$

8) 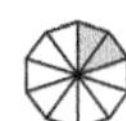 $\frac{2}{10}$

9)  $\frac{1}{8}$

10) 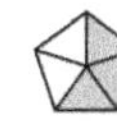 $\frac{3}{5}$

EXERCISE 11

1) $\frac{5}{6}$

2) 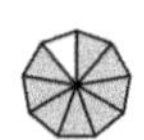 $\frac{8}{9}$

3)  $\frac{7}{9}$

4) $\frac{6}{10}$

5) $\frac{7}{8}$

6)  $\frac{8}{10}$

7) $\frac{2}{5}$

8) $\frac{6}{7}$

9) $\frac{5}{7}$

10) $\frac{3}{7}$

EXERCISE 12

1) 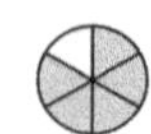 $\frac{5}{6}$

2) $\frac{7}{8}$

3) $\frac{1}{3}$

4) $\frac{4}{5}$

5)  $\frac{2}{7}$

6)  $\frac{1}{4}$

7) $\frac{3}{4}$

8) $\frac{5}{7}$

9) $\frac{3}{5}$

10)  $\frac{3}{6}$

EXERCISE 13

1) $\frac{6}{8}$

2) 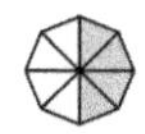 $\frac{4}{8}$

3) 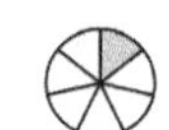 $\frac{1}{7}$

4)  $\frac{2}{10}$

5) $\frac{4}{9}$

6) 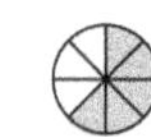 $\frac{5}{8}$

7) $\frac{1}{5}$

8) $\frac{3}{8}$

9) $\frac{5}{9}$

10) $\frac{3}{6}$

EXERCISE 14

1) 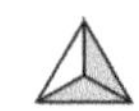 $\frac{2}{3}$

2)  $\frac{2}{10}$

3) $\frac{5}{6}$

4) $\frac{3}{4}$

5) $\frac{1}{5}$

6)  $\frac{1}{9}$

7) $\frac{4}{8}$

8) $\frac{1}{8}$

9) $\frac{2}{4}$

10) $\frac{5}{8}$

EXERCISE 15

1) $\frac{7}{10}$

2) $\frac{1}{2}$

3)  $\frac{3}{5}$

4) 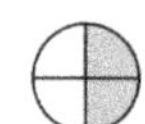 $\frac{2}{4}$

5) 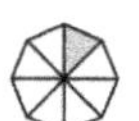 $\frac{1}{8}$

6) 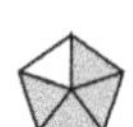 $\frac{4}{5}$

7) $\frac{1}{10}$

8) $\frac{5}{8}$

9)  $\frac{2}{5}$

10) 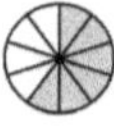 $\frac{6}{10}$

EXERCISE 166

1)		$\frac{8}{9}$	6)	 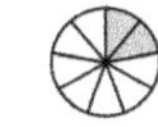	$\frac{2}{9}$
2)		$\frac{9}{10}$	7)		$\frac{1}{8}$
3)		$\frac{6}{9}$	8)		$\frac{1}{4}$
4)	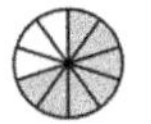	$\frac{7}{10}$	9)		$\frac{4}{8}$
5)		$\frac{2}{5}$	10)		$\frac{2}{7}$

EXERCISE 17

1)		$\frac{7}{8}$	6)		$\frac{1}{3}$
2)		$\frac{1}{6}$	7)		$\frac{3}{10}$
3)		$\frac{1}{10}$	8)		$\frac{2}{7}$
4)		$\frac{2}{8}$	9)	 	$\frac{3}{7}$
5)		$\frac{2}{10}$	10)		$\frac{3}{8}$

EXERCISE 18

1)		$\frac{4}{5}$	6)	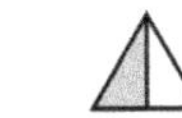	$\frac{1}{2}$
2)		$\frac{4}{10}$	7)	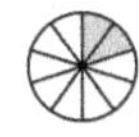	$\frac{2}{10}$
3)		$\frac{1}{9}$	8)		$\frac{6}{8}$
4)		$\frac{9}{10}$	9)	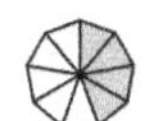	$\frac{4}{9}$
5)		$\frac{5}{7}$	10)		$\frac{2}{6}$

EXERCISE 19

1)	 	$\frac{2}{10}$	6)		$\frac{3}{7}$
2)		$\frac{7}{9}$	7)		$\frac{3}{5}$
3)	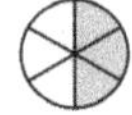	$\frac{3}{6}$	8)		$\frac{4}{6}$
4)	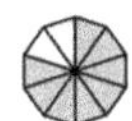	$\frac{8}{10}$	9)		$\frac{4}{5}$
5)		$\frac{1}{5}$	10)		$\frac{5}{9}$

EXERCISE 20

1)		$\frac{6}{10}$	6)	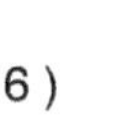	$\frac{6}{7}$
2)	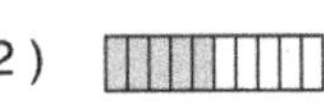	$\frac{5}{10}$	7)	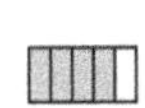	$\frac{4}{5}$
3)	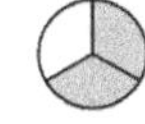	$\frac{2}{3}$	8)		$\frac{7}{8}$
4)	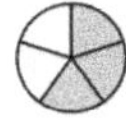	$\frac{3}{5}$	9)		$\frac{1}{2}$
5)		$\frac{8}{9}$	10)		$\frac{4}{7}$

EXERCISE 21

1)		$\frac{8}{10}$	6)		$\frac{3}{8}$
2)	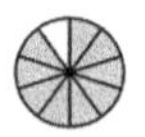	$\frac{9}{10}$	7)		$\frac{1}{3}$
3)		$\frac{2}{6}$	8)		$\frac{8}{9}$
4)		$\frac{3}{6}$	9)		$\frac{4}{10}$
5)		$\frac{1}{9}$	10)		$\frac{1}{2}$

EXERCISE 22

1)		$\frac{6}{7}$	6)	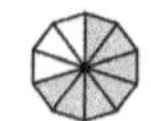	$\frac{7}{10}$
2)		$\frac{5}{9}$	7)		$\frac{1}{3}$
3)		$\frac{7}{8}$	8)		$\frac{7}{9}$
4)		$\frac{4}{6}$	9)		$\frac{6}{8}$
5)		$\frac{1}{10}$	10)		$\frac{1}{9}$

EXERCISE 23

1)	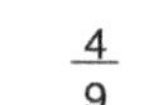	$\frac{4}{9}$	6)	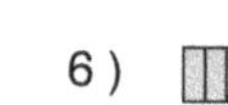 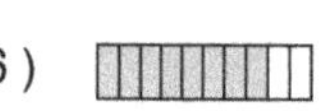	$\frac{8}{10}$
2)	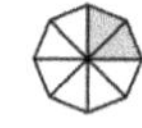	$\frac{2}{8}$	7)		$\frac{7}{9}$
3)	 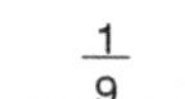	$\frac{1}{9}$	8)	 	$\frac{4}{10}$
4)	 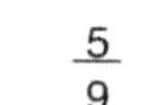	$\frac{5}{9}$	9)		$\frac{2}{6}$
5)	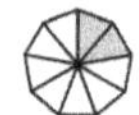  	$\frac{2}{9}$	10)	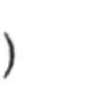 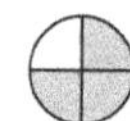 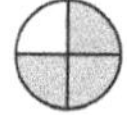 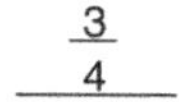	$\frac{3}{4}$

EXERCISE 24

1)	 	$\frac{6}{10}$	6)	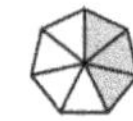	$\frac{3}{7}$
2)		$\frac{2}{5}$	7)	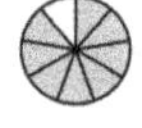	$\frac{8}{9}$
3)		$\frac{6}{9}$	8)		$\frac{4}{7}$
4)		$\frac{5}{10}$	9)		$\frac{2}{8}$
5)	 	$\frac{3}{4}$	10)	 	$\frac{2}{6}$

EXERCISE 25

1)		$\frac{3}{4}$	6)	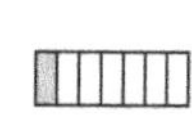	$\frac{1}{7}$
2)		$\frac{8}{9}$	7)		$\frac{1}{2}$
3)		$\frac{6}{9}$	8)		$\frac{1}{6}$
4)		$\frac{6}{10}$	9)		$\frac{2}{3}$
5)		$\frac{1}{9}$	10)		$\frac{2}{7}$

EXERCISE 26

1)		$\frac{1}{3}$	6)	 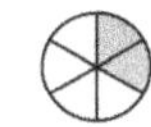	$\frac{2}{6}$
2)		$\frac{2}{3}$	7)	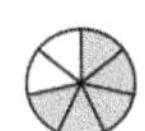	$\frac{5}{7}$
3)		$\frac{2}{10}$	8)		$\frac{8}{9}$
4)		$\frac{1}{5}$	9)		$\frac{4}{5}$
5)		$\frac{5}{10}$	10)		$\frac{3}{10}$

EXERCISE 27

1)	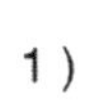 	$\frac{1}{7}$	6)	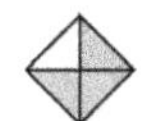	$\frac{3}{4}$
2)		$\frac{3}{5}$	7)		$\frac{7}{8}$
3)	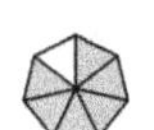	$\frac{6}{7}$	8)		$\frac{3}{6}$
4)	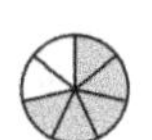	$\frac{5}{7}$	9)		$\frac{6}{8}$
5)		$\frac{1}{5}$	10)		$\frac{1}{9}$

EXERCISE 28

1)		$\frac{3}{10}$	6)		$\frac{1}{2}$
2)		$\frac{2}{5}$	7)		$\frac{5}{6}$
3)		$\frac{4}{8}$	8)		$\frac{4}{7}$
4)	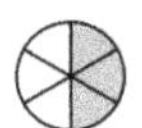	$\frac{3}{6}$	9)		$\frac{2}{9}$
5)		$\frac{6}{8}$	10)		$\frac{6}{10}$

EXERCISE 29

1)		$\frac{5}{7}$	6)		$\frac{3}{4}$
2)		$\frac{2}{9}$	7)		$\frac{5}{8}$
3)		$\frac{5}{9}$	8)		$\frac{1}{3}$
4)		$\frac{2}{3}$	9)		$\frac{2}{7}$
5)		$\frac{7}{8}$	10)		$\frac{1}{10}$

EXERCISE 30

1)		$\frac{7}{8}$	6)		$\frac{8}{10}$
2)		$\frac{4}{9}$	7)		$\frac{5}{10}$
3)	 	$\frac{4}{8}$	8)		$\frac{4}{5}$
4)	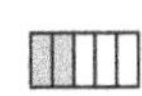	$\frac{2}{5}$	9)	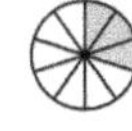	$\frac{3}{10}$
5)	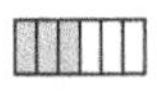	$\frac{3}{6}$	10)	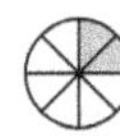	$\frac{2}{8}$

EXERCISE 31

1) $\frac{2}{4}$

2) $\frac{3}{4}$

3) $\frac{1}{10}$

4) $\frac{2}{10}$

5) 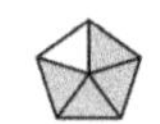 $\frac{4}{5}$

6) 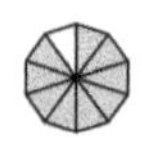 $\frac{9}{10}$

7) $\frac{7}{10}$

8) $\frac{6}{9}$

9) $\frac{5}{10}$

10) 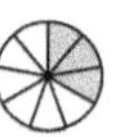 $\frac{3}{9}$

EXERCISE 32

1)  $\frac{4}{9}$

2) $\frac{4}{7}$

3) 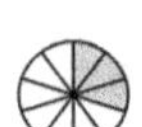 $\frac{3}{10}$

4)  $\frac{2}{6}$

5)  $\frac{3}{9}$

6) $\frac{1}{8}$

7)  $\frac{9}{10}$

8)  $\frac{5}{8}$

9) 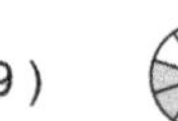 $\frac{8}{10}$

10) 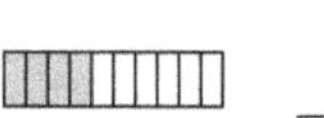 $\frac{4}{10}$

EXERCISE 33

1) $\frac{6}{9}$

2)  $\frac{1}{4}$

3)  $\frac{1}{9}$

4) 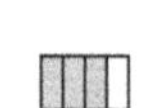 $\frac{3}{4}$

5) 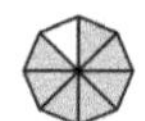 $\frac{7}{8}$

6) 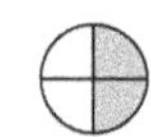 $\frac{2}{4}$

7) 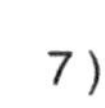  $\frac{2}{3}$

8) 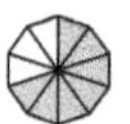 $\frac{7}{10}$

9) $\frac{3}{9}$

10) $\frac{3}{10}$

EXERCISE 34

1) 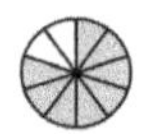 $\frac{8}{10}$

2) $\frac{6}{9}$

3) $\frac{4}{6}$

4) $\frac{1}{2}$

5)  $\frac{4}{9}$

6) $\frac{1}{3}$

7) $\frac{2}{7}$

8) $\frac{1}{7}$

9) $\frac{3}{9}$

10) $\frac{6}{8}$

EXERCISE 35

1) $\frac{1}{9}$

2)  $\frac{8}{9}$

3)  $\frac{6}{9}$

4)  $\frac{6}{8}$

5)  $\frac{1}{6}$

6) $\frac{1}{7}$

7) $\frac{3}{10}$

8) $\frac{1}{4}$

9) $\frac{4}{6}$

10) $\frac{3}{4}$

EXERCISE 36

1)  $\frac{3}{5}$

2) $\frac{4}{9}$

3) $\frac{1}{10}$

4) $\frac{3}{9}$

5) $\frac{2}{3}$

6) 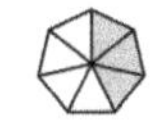 $\frac{3}{7}$

7) $\frac{8}{10}$

8) $\frac{6}{10}$

9) $\frac{1}{7}$

10) 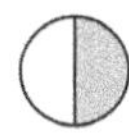 $\frac{1}{2}$

EXERCISE 37

1) $\frac{5}{6}$

2) $\frac{5}{7}$

3) 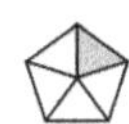 $\frac{1}{5}$

4) $\frac{1}{2}$

5) 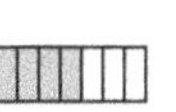 $\frac{4}{7}$

6) $\frac{2}{5}$

7) 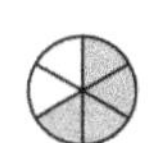 $\frac{4}{6}$

8) 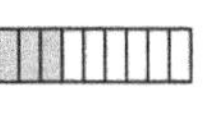 $\frac{4}{10}$

9) $\frac{2}{3}$

10)  $\frac{9}{10}$

EXERCISE 38

1) 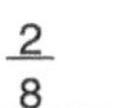 $\frac{2}{8}$

2) 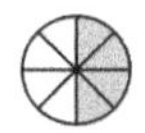 $\frac{4}{8}$

3)  $\frac{7}{9}$

4) 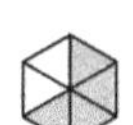 $\frac{4}{6}$

5)  $\frac{6}{9}$

6) 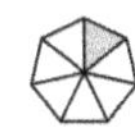 $\frac{1}{7}$

7) 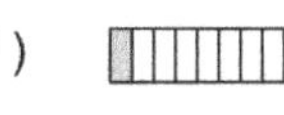 $\frac{1}{8}$

8)  $\frac{3}{5}$

9) $\frac{3}{10}$

10) $\frac{6}{10}$

EXERCISE 39

1)  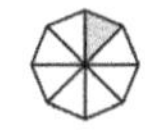 $\frac{1}{8}$

2) 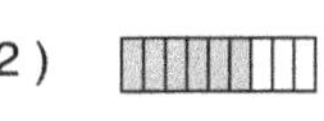 $\frac{6}{9}$

3)  $\frac{5}{10}$

4) 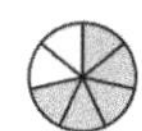 $\frac{5}{7}$

5)  $\frac{6}{7}$

6)  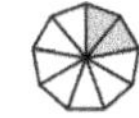 $\frac{2}{9}$

7)  $\frac{4}{8}$

8) $\frac{8}{9}$

9) 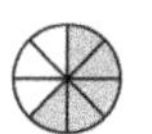 $\frac{5}{8}$

10) $\frac{4}{10}$

EXERCISE 40

1) $\frac{2}{6}$

2) 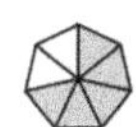 $\frac{5}{7}$

3)  $\frac{2}{8}$

4) $\frac{1}{10}$

5) 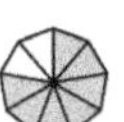 $\frac{7}{9}$

6) 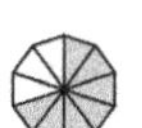 $\frac{7}{10}$

7)  $\frac{2}{7}$

8)  $\frac{1}{8}$

9) $\frac{9}{10}$

10) 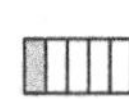 $\frac{1}{5}$

EXERCISE 1

1) $\frac{5}{12} + \frac{6}{12} = \frac{11}{12}$

2) $\frac{2}{12} + \frac{6}{12} = \frac{8}{12}$

3) $\frac{4}{11} + \frac{6}{11} = \frac{10}{11}$

4) $\frac{1}{12} + \frac{5}{12} = \frac{6}{12}$

5) $\frac{2}{6} + \frac{3}{6} = \frac{5}{6}$

6) $\frac{1}{9} + \frac{3}{9} = \frac{4}{9}$

EXERCISE 2

1) $\frac{1}{6} + \frac{3}{6} = \frac{4}{6}$

2) $\frac{1}{3} + \frac{1}{3} = \frac{2}{3}$

3) $\frac{4}{12} + \frac{7}{12} = \frac{11}{12}$

4) $\frac{1}{4} + \frac{2}{4} = \frac{3}{4}$

5) $\frac{3}{12} + \frac{6}{12} = \frac{9}{12}$

6) $\frac{4}{10} + \frac{4}{10} = \frac{8}{10}$

EXERCISE 3

1) $\frac{1}{4} + \frac{2}{4} = \frac{3}{4}$

2) $\frac{2}{9} + \frac{6}{9} = \frac{8}{9}$

3) $\frac{2}{12} + \frac{2}{12} = \frac{4}{12}$

4) $\frac{2}{5} + \frac{2}{5} = \frac{4}{5}$

5) $\frac{1}{12} + \frac{7}{12} = \frac{8}{12}$

6) $\frac{1}{10} + \frac{1}{10} = \frac{2}{10}$

EXERCISE 4

1) $\frac{8}{10} - \frac{1}{5} = \frac{8}{10} - \frac{2}{10} = \frac{6}{10} = \frac{3}{5}$

2) $\frac{2}{4} - \frac{1}{5} = \frac{10}{20} - \frac{4}{20} = \frac{6}{20} = \frac{3}{10}$

3) $\frac{7}{10} - \frac{2}{4} = \frac{14}{20} - \frac{10}{20} = \frac{4}{20} = \frac{1}{5}$

4) $\frac{4}{5} - \frac{1}{2} = \frac{8}{10} - \frac{5}{10} = \frac{3}{10}$

5) $\frac{4}{5} - \frac{3}{4} = \frac{16}{20} - \frac{15}{20} = \frac{1}{20}$

6) $\frac{1}{2} - \frac{3}{10} = \frac{5}{10} - \frac{3}{10} = \frac{2}{10} = \frac{1}{5}$

EXERCISE 5

1) $\frac{8}{10} - \frac{2}{4} = \frac{16}{20} - \frac{10}{20} = \frac{6}{20} = \frac{3}{10}$

2) $\frac{4}{5} - \frac{4}{10} = \frac{8}{10} - \frac{4}{10} = \frac{4}{10} = \frac{2}{5}$

3) $\frac{3}{5} - \frac{1}{2} = \frac{6}{10} - \frac{5}{10} = \frac{1}{10}$

4) $\frac{2}{3} - \frac{1}{2} = \frac{4}{6} - \frac{3}{6} = \frac{1}{6}$

5) $\frac{1}{2} - \frac{1}{5} = \frac{5}{10} - \frac{2}{10} = \frac{3}{10}$

6) $\frac{1}{2} - \frac{1}{4} = \frac{2}{4} - \frac{1}{4} = \frac{1}{4}$

EXERCISE 6

1) $\frac{5}{10} - \frac{1}{3} = \frac{15}{30} - \frac{10}{30} = \frac{5}{30} = \frac{1}{6}$

2) $\frac{3}{5} - \frac{2}{10} = \frac{6}{10} - \frac{2}{10} = \frac{4}{10} = \frac{2}{5}$

3) $\frac{1}{2} - \frac{1}{4} = \frac{2}{4} - \frac{1}{4} = \frac{1}{4}$

4) $\frac{2}{3} - \frac{1}{2} = \frac{4}{6} - \frac{3}{6} = \frac{1}{6}$

5) $\frac{9}{10} - \frac{1}{3} = \frac{27}{30} - \frac{10}{30} = \frac{17}{30}$

6) $\frac{1}{2} - \frac{2}{10} = \frac{5}{10} - \frac{2}{10} = \frac{3}{10}$

Visit
BABY PROFESSOR
EDUCATION KIDS
www.BabyProfessorBooks.com
to download Free Baby Professor eBooks
and view our catalog of new and exciting
Children's Books

www.ingramcontent.com/pod-product-compliance
Lightning Source LLC
LaVergne TN
LVHW060826170826
845678LV00010B/1915
* 9 7 9 8 8 6 9 4 4 2 0 1 7 *